COLLECTIONS

Teacher's Resource Book
Kindergarten

Orlando   Boston   Dallas   Chicago   San Diego

Visit *The Learning Site!*
www.harcourtschool.com

Copyright © by Harcourt, Inc.

All rights reserved. No part of this publication may be reproduced or transmitted in any form or by any means, electronic or mechanical, including photocopy, recording, or any information storage and retrieval system.

Teachers using COLLECTIONS may photocopy complete pages in sufficient quantities for classroom use only and not for resale.

HARCOURT and the Harcourt Logo are trademarks of Harcourt, Inc.

Acknowledgements

For permission to reprint copyrighted material, grateful acknowledgment is made to the following sources:

Harcourt Inc.: Illustration from *Look Closer* by Brian and Rebecca Wildsmith. Copyright © 1993 by Brian and Rebecca Wildsmith.

North-South Books Inc., New York: Illustrations from *Five Little Ducks: An Old Rhyme*, illustrated by Pamela Paparone. Illustrations copyright © 1995 by Pamela Paparone.

Simon & Schuster Books for Young Readers, Simon & Schuster Children's Publishing Division: Illustration by Mick Inkpen from *Jasper's Beanstalk* by Nick Butterworth. Illustrations copyright © 1993 by Mick Inkpen.

Printed in the United States of America

ISBN 0-15-313427-5

2 3 4 5 6 7 8 9 10 054 2002 2001 2000

Contents

About This Book 1

Family Letters 2

Take-Home Books

"6 Monkeys" 3
"Me" 5
"The Zoo" 7
"Lunch" 9
"Toys" 11
"Pig's Party" 13
"The House" 15
"Here We Go!" 17
"The Cake" 19
"Apple Animals" 21
"My Baby" 23
"Help!" 25
"Jump In" 27
"My Boat!" 29
"The Ostrich" 31
"What Can You See?" 33
"The North Pole" 35
"We Like What We See" 37
"The Movie Theater" 39
"Best Friend" 41
"What You Have" 43
"Can I Have It?" 45
"The Goose" 47

Contents

"My Garden" 49
"The Surprise" 51
"Sam and Pam" 53
"The Missing Cap" 55
"The Boat Trip" 57
"The Fish" 59
"Look at That!" 61

Letter and Sound Charts 63

Character Cutouts

The Alphabet 89
"The Hare and the Tortoise" 94
"Bought Me a Cat" 95
"The Gingerbread Man" 97
"The Three Billy-Goats Gruff" 99
"Franklin in the Dark" 100
"Mother, Mother, I Want Another" 102
"Coyote and Turtle" 104
"Henny Penny" 105
"The Three Little Pigs" 107
"Anansi and the Biggest, Sweetest Melon" 108
"My Pet Spider" 110
"If You Ever" 112

Big Book Activity Cards 113

Reproducible Resources 127

About This Book

★ Take-Home Books

The thirty *Take-Home Books* reinforce the target letters or phonograms taught in each theme. Each child needs a copy of the *Take-Home Books* to read with family members.

★ Letter and Sound Charts

Twenty-six *Letter and Sound Charts* can be used for small-group read-alongs. Use them to assess children's progress in letter recognition and print awareness.

★ Character Cutouts

Character Cutouts can be used to retell stories, songs, and poems and support other activities for specific selections in the *Read-Aloud Anthology*.

★ Big Book Activity Cards

Big Book Activity Cards provide opportunities for independent responses to the *Big Books*. They also require children to follow directions, carry a task through to completion, and integrate story knowledge with a hands-on activity.

★ Reproducible Resources

These blackline masters will help you actively involve children in oral language, listening, and cooperative learning tasks.

Date:_____

Dear Family Members,

The kindergarten program provides many opportunities for children to learn literacy skills while sharing what they know with their classmates. Teaching children to become successful readers and writers involves cooperation between the school and home. During the year, there will be times when requests will be made for children to bring to school items or information related to what they are learning. Thank you for your help.

Sincerely,

_____

• •

Date:_____

Dear Family Members,

We are doing a project at school and need some items to complete the activity. Please have your child bring in the following by_____.

_____
_____
_____
_____
_____
_____

Thank you,

_____

6 Monkeys

by _____

2 _onkeys

Dear Family Members,

This Take-Home Book contains a word that begins with a letter your child is learning about. After reading the story with your child, encourage him or her to read it to you. Then discuss your child's favorite activities at school.

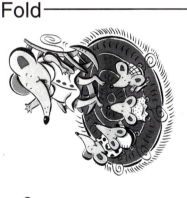

Harcourt

5 _onkeys

Directions: Help children cut and fold the book.
Use with *Teacher's Edition* volume 1, page T123.

TAKE HOME BOOK 3

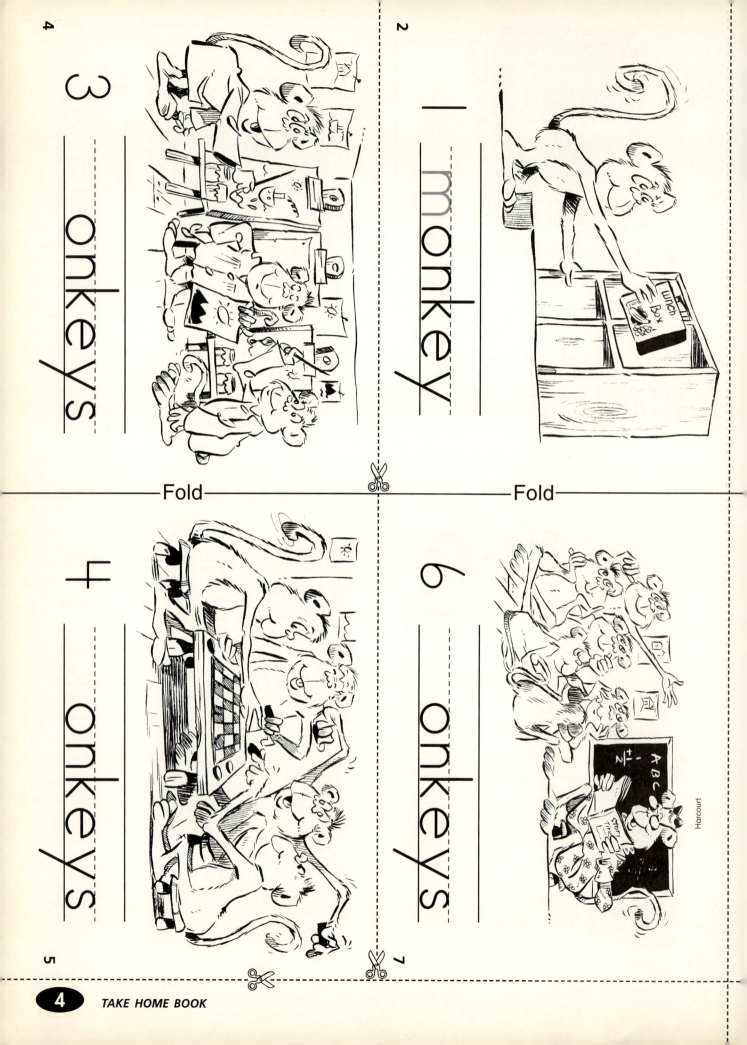

_____ ingers

by _____

---Fold--- ---Fold---

Dear Family Members,
This Take-Home Book contains words that begin with letters your child is learning about. After reading the story with your child, encourage him or her to read it to you. Then have your child draw a picture of an activity he or she enjoys doing.

Harcourt

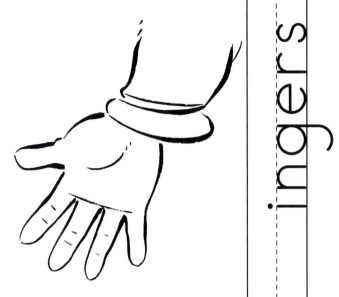

_____ ootball

Directions: Help children cut and fold the book.
Use with *Teacher's Edition* volume 1, page T155.

TAKE HOME BOOK

4

outh

2

face

—Fold—

ence

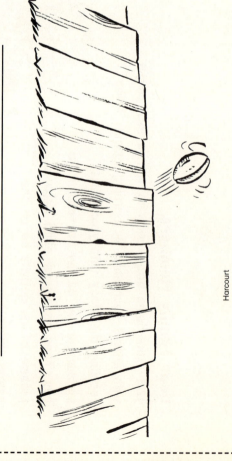

eet

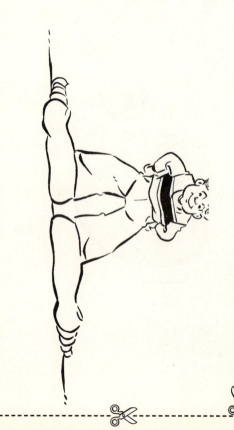

5

6 TAKE HOME BOOK

The Zoo

by _____

3

___ird

the

Fold

___onkey

the

6

Dear Family Members,
This Take-Home Book contains words that begin with letters your child is learning about. After reading the story with your child, encourage him or her to read it to you. Then have your child name some of his or her favorite zoo animals. Take turns telling facts you both know about any of the animals.

Harcourt

8

Directions: Help children cut and fold the book.
Use with *Teacher's Edition* volume 1, page T197.

TAKE HOME BOOK 7

4

the ___ox

the ___bear 2

the ___uffalo

the ___ish 7

5

8 TAKE HOME BOOK

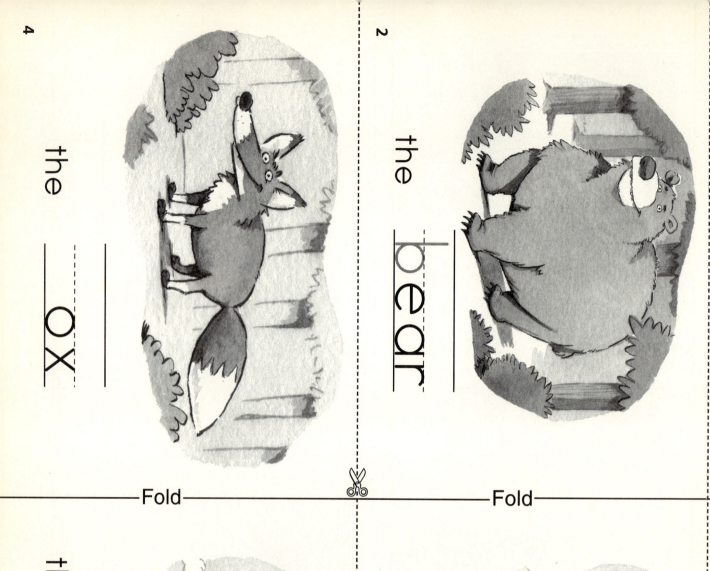
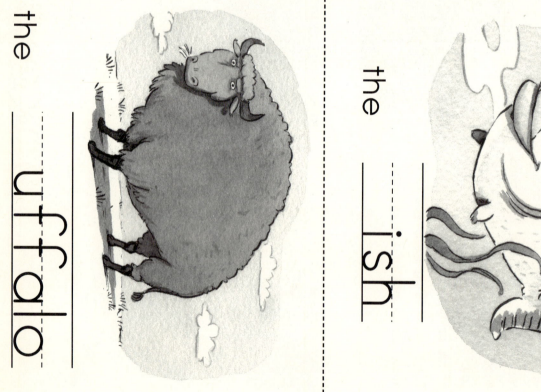

Lunch

by _____

Dear Family Members,

This Take-Home Book contains words that begin with letters your child is learning about. After reading the story with your child, encourage him or her to read it to you. Then have your child name some of his or her favorite lunch foods. Invite him or her to draw pictures of the foods. Talk about the sound your child hears at the beginning of each food name.

the _____oup

the _____anana

Directions: Help children cut and fold the book.
Use with *Teacher's Edition* volume 1, page T227.

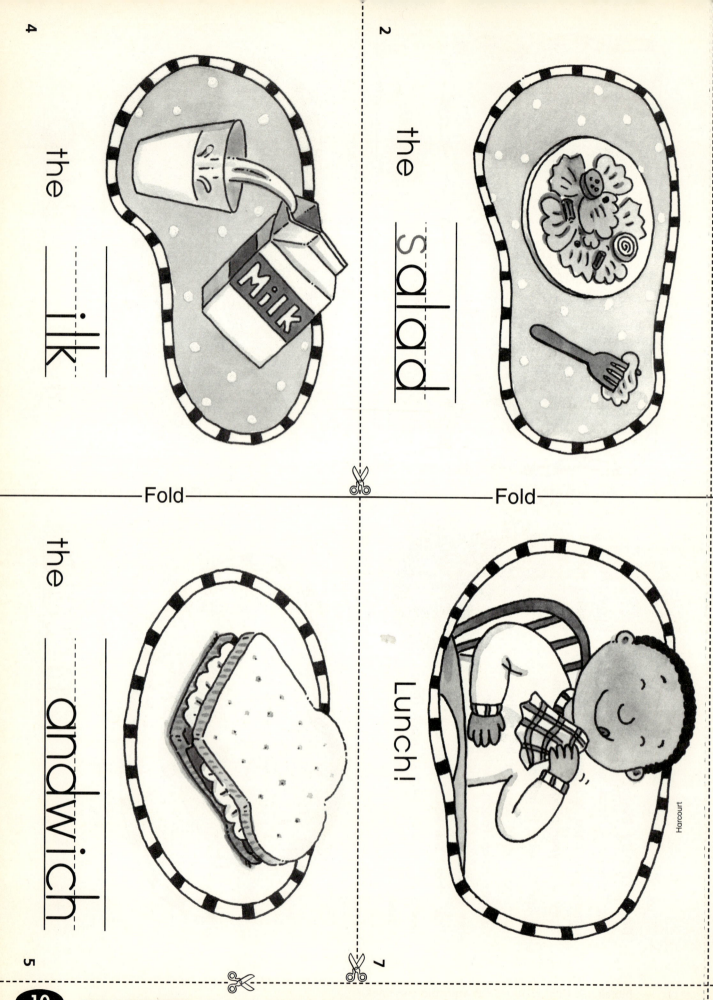

Toys

by _____

2 ___ets

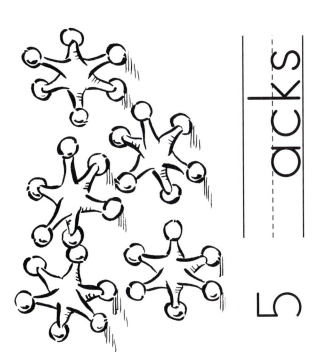

5 ___acks

Dear Family Members,

This Take-Home Book contains words that begin with letters your child is learning about. After reading the story with your child, encourage him or her to read it to you. Then help your child draw and write about a toy he or she would like to have.

Directions: Help children cut and fold the book.
Use with *Teacher's Edition* volume 1, page T269.

TAKE HOME BOOK

4

1 jack-in-the-box

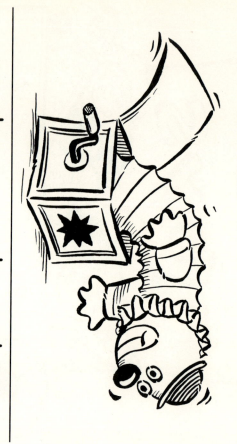

2
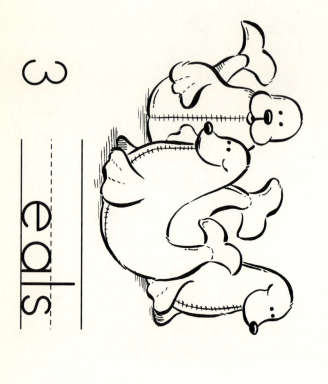

3 ___ eals

—Fold— ✂ —Fold—

6 ___ agnets

4 ___ alls

TAKE HOME BOOK

Pig's Party

by

the ___arrot

---Fold--- ---Fold---

Dear Family Members,
This Take-Home Book contains words that begin with letters your child is learning about. After reading the story with your child, encourage him or her to read it to you. Then help your child make an invitation to an imaginary party he or she would like to have.

Harcourt

the ___eacock

Directions: Help children cut and fold the book.
Use with *Teacher's Edition* volume 1, page T301.

TAKE HOME BOOK   13

4

the ____ ear

2

the p i g

—Fold— ✂ —Fold—

the ____ ox

5

the ____ a r t y

7

14 TAKE HOME BOOK

The House

by _____

I have a ___eep.

3

Dear Family Members,
This Take-Home Book contains words that begin with letters your child is learning about. After reading the story with your child, encourage him or her to read it to you. Talk about other things Hippo might add to his house, and ask your child to listen for the beginning sound in each word.

8

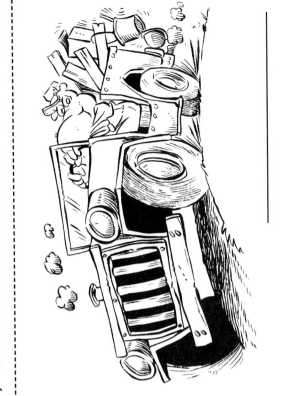

I have a ___an.

6

Directions: Help children cut and fold the book.
Use with *Teacher's Edition* volume 1, page T345.

TAKE HOME BOOK 15

4

I have a _athtub_.

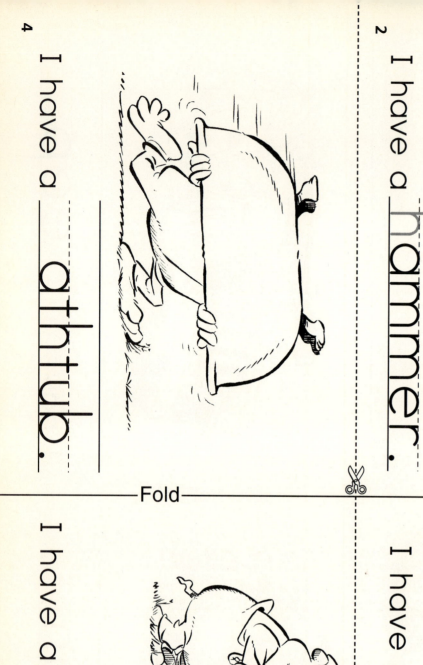

2

I have a _hammer_.

—Fold—

—Fold—

I have a _ouse_!

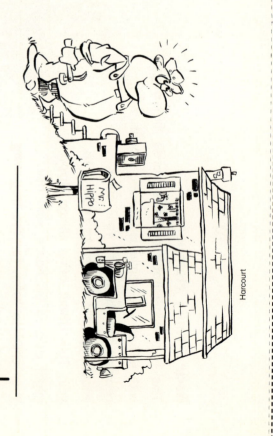

I have a _ailbox_.

7

5

TAKE HOME BOOK

Here We Go!

by _____

3

I have the ____ uck.

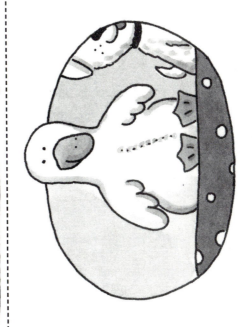

Dear Family Members,

This Take-Home Book contains words that begin with letters your child is learning about. After reading the story with your child, encourage him or her to read it to you. Talk about other toys the girl might put in her wagon, and ask your child to listen for the beginning sound in each word.

8

I have the ____ ear.

6

Directions: Help children cut and fold the book.
Use with *Teacher's Edition* volume 1, page T375.

TAKE HOME BOOK 17

2

I have the dog.

4

I have the orse.

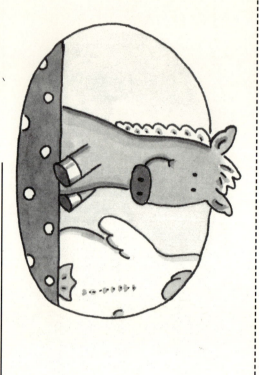

I have the onkey.

Here we go!

5

TAKE HOME BOOK

The Cake

by _____

I have a __ og.

Dear Family Members,
This Take-Home Book contains words that begin with *c* and *d*. After reading the story with your child, encourage him or her to read it to you. Then play a birthday-party game. In a gift box, hide a familiar object whose name begins with the same sound as *cap* or *dad*. Give your child hints for him or her to guess the object.

I have a __ oll.

Directions: Help children cut and fold the book.
Use with *Teacher's Edition* volume 1, page T419.

4

I have a __ar.

2

I have a cat.

—Fold—

Fold

I have a cake!

I have a __ap.

7

5

20 TAKE HOME BOOK

Apple Animals

by ____

___pple
dog

3

___lligator
apple

6

Dear Family Members,

This Take-Home Book contains words that begin with letters your child is learning about. After reading the story with your child, encourage him or her to read it to you. Invite your child to help you make one of the animals shown, and share it with other family members.

Harcourt

8

Directions: Help children cut and fold the book.
Use with *Teacher's Edition* volume 1, page T451.

TAKE HOME BOOK   21

4

apple bunny

2

apple bird

Fold

Fold

apple at

apple animal

5

7

TAKE HOME BOOK

My Baby

by _____

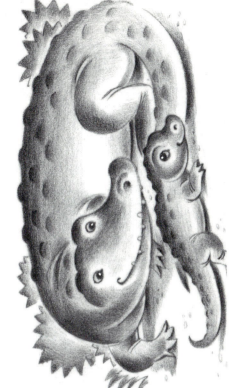

I have my _____lligator.

3

Dear Family Members,

This Take-Home Book contains words that begin with letters your child is learning about. After reading the story with your child, encourage him or her to read it to you. Then start an animal dictionary together. Help your child choose an animal that starts with the letter *a*. Then invite him or her to illustrate the animal and label it. Continue with other letters.

Harcourt

8

I have my _____amel.

6

Directions: Help children cut and fold the book.
Use with *Teacher's Edition* volume 1, page T493.

TAKE HOME BOOK   23

2

I have my turtle.

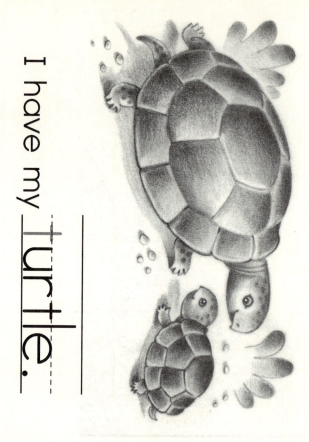

4

I have my turkey.

7

I have my tiger.

5

I have my fox.

24 TAKE HOME BOOK

Help!

by _____

Dear Family Members,

This Take-Home Book contains words that begin with letters your child is learning about. After reading the story with your child, encourage him or her to read it to you. Then talk about other ways the animals may have gotten the kitten down from the tree.

Harcourt

8

Can ____lligator help?

3

Can ____lephant help?

6

Directions: Help children cut and fold the book.
Use with *Teacher's Edition* volume 1, page T523.

TAKE HOME BOOK 25

2

Can turtle help?

4

Can Tiger help?

7

unny can help.

5

Can Hippo help?

Jump In

by

The ___og can jump in.

The ___ak can jump in.

Dear Family Members,
This Take-Home Book contains words that begin with letters your child is learning about. After reading the story with your child, encourage him or her to read it to you. Then talk about the size of each animal, and invite your child to order them from smallest to biggest.

Directions: Help children cut and fold the book.
Use with *Teacher's Edition* volume 2, page T41.

TAKE HOME BOOK

My Boat!

by _____

I like you, ____at.

I like you, ____ak.

Dear Family Members,
This Take-Home Book contains words that begin with letters your child is learning about. After reading the story with your child, encourage him or her to read it to you. Then experiment together to test objects that sink and float.

Harcourt

Directions: Help children cut and fold the book.
Use with *Teacher's Edition* volume 2, page T73.

TAKE HOME BOOK

2   I like you, horse.

4   I like you, octopus.

My boat!

7   I like you, pig.

30 TAKE HOME BOOK

The Ostrich

by _____

You like the ___strich.

3

Dear Family Members,

This Take-Home Book contains words that begin with letters your child is learning about. After reading the story with your child, encourage him or her to read it to you. Then talk about animals you might see at the zoo.

Harcourt

8

I like the ___ctopus.

6

Directions: Help children cut and fold the book.
Use with *Teacher's Edition* volume 2, page T97.

TAKE HOME BOOK **31**

4

I like the __gorilla__.

2

I like the __Zebra__.

You like the __ostrich__.

You like the __Strich__.

32 TAKE HOME BOOK

What Can You See?

What Can You See?

by _____

I see a _____angaroo.

I see a _____enguin.

Dear Family Members,

This Take-Home Book contains words that begin with letters your child is learning about. After reading the story with your child, encourage him or her to read it to you. Then talk about the different kinds of animals that live near your neighborhood.

Harcourt

Directions: Help children cut and fold the book.
Use with *Teacher's Edition* volume 2, page T141.

TAKE HOME BOOK

4

I see a __onkey.__

2

I see a __zebra.__

—Fold—

7

I see a __ook.__

5

I see a __eal.__

34 TAKE HOME BOOK

The North Pole
by

I can see the igloo.

3

I can see the walrus.

6

Dear Family Members,
This Take-Home Book contains words that begin with letters your child is learning about. After reading the story with your child, encourage him or her to read it to you. Then talk about what happens in winter in your neighborhood.

Harcourt

8

Directions: Help children cut and fold the book.
Use with *Teacher's Edition* volume 2, page T171.

TAKE HOME BOOK 35

4

I can see the **cat**.

2

I can see the **moon**.

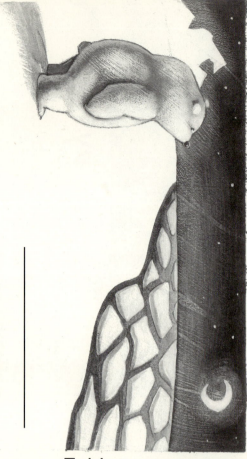

I can see the **dog**.

I can see the **sun**.

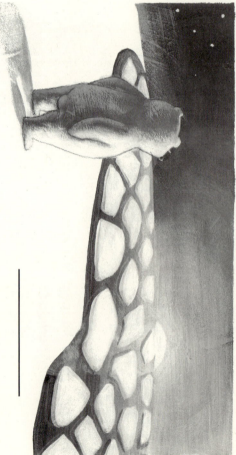

Harcourt

7

5

36 TAKE HOME BOOK

We Like What We See

by _____

I see the _____ alrus.

Dear Family Members,

This Take-Home Book contains words that begin with letters your child is learning about. After reading the story with your child, encourage him or her to read it to you. Then make a list of all the places your child can see his or her reflection.

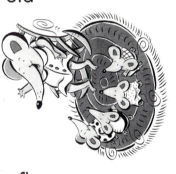

Harcourt

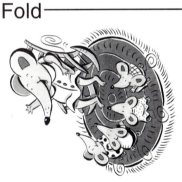

I see the _____ orse.

Directions: Help children cut and fold the book.
Use with *Teacher's Edition* volume 2, page T195.

4

I see the tiger.

2

I see the iguana.

— Fold —

— Fold —

I see the wolf.

We like what we see.

5

7

38 TAKE HOME BOOK

The Movie Theater

by _____

I have ___ickets.

3

Dear Family Members,
This Take-Home Book contains words that begin with letters your child is learning about. After reading the story with your child, encourage him or her to read it to you. Then discuss some of your child's favorite movies and the characters in them.

Harcourt

8

I see the ___ain.

6

Directions: Help children cut and fold the book.
Use with *Teacher's Edition* volume 2, page T239.

TAKE HOME BOOK 39

2

I see the window.

4

I see the ood.

I have the mbrella.

7

I have opcorn.

5

40 TAKE HOME BOOK

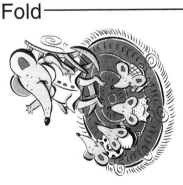

Best Friend

by _____

your ___unch box

3

Dear Family Members,
This Take-Home Book contains words that begin with letters your child is learning about. After reading the story with your child, encourage him or her to read it to you. Then discuss what the bear does in the story and have your child name things that he or she likes to do with friends.

8

your ___mbrella

6

Directions: Help children cut and fold the book.
Use with *Teacher's Edition* volume 2, page T271.

TAKE HOME BOOK 41

4

your __ ike

2

your backpack

—Fold— —Fold—

your best friend

your __ ion

5   7

42 TAKE HOME BOOK

What You Have

_____ by _____

I like your _____ idea.

Harcourt

Dear Family Members,
This Take-Home Book contains words that begin with letters your child is learning about. After reading the story with your child, encourage him or her to read it to you. Then make a list of your child's favorite things.

You have a _____ cat.

Directions: Help children cut and fold the book.
Use with *Teacher's Edition* volume 2, page T295.

TAKE HOME BOOK 43

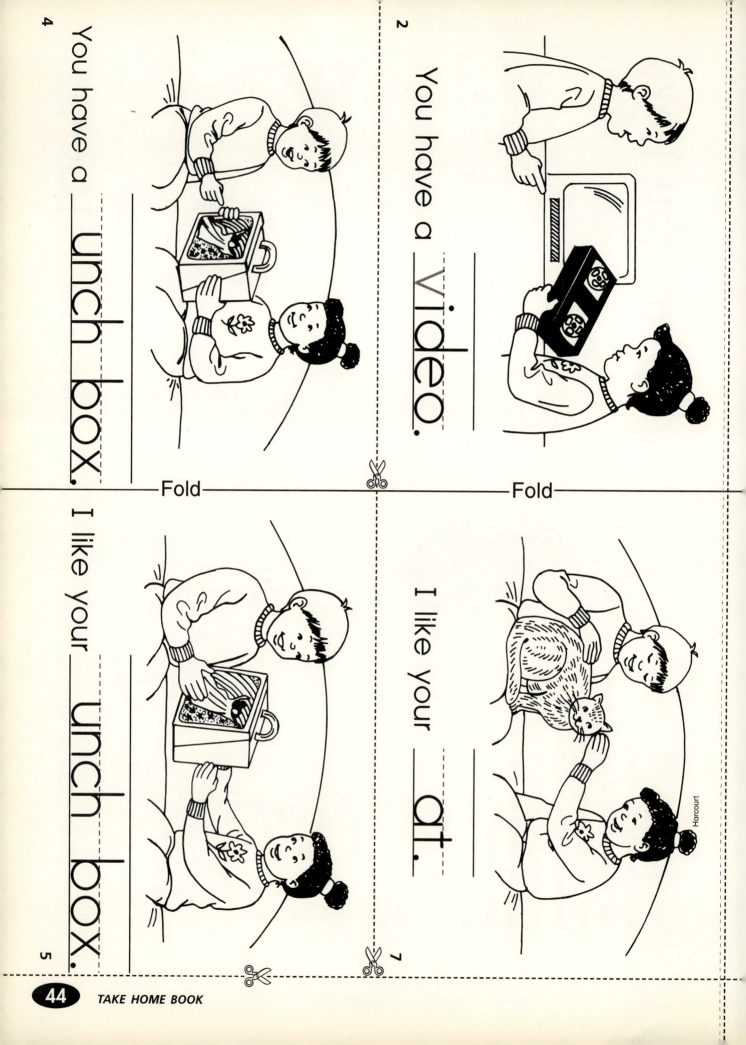

2 You have a video.

4 You have a **l**unch box.

I like your **c**at.

I like your **l**unch box.

44 TAKE HOME BOOK

Can I Have It?

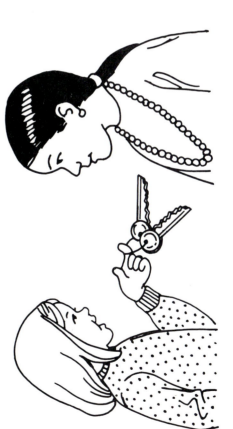

My ___ ase?

My ___ eys?

3

6

―Fold―――――――――――Fold―

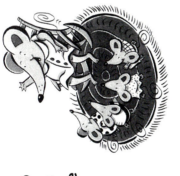

Dear Family Members,
This Take-Home Book contains words that begin with letters your child is learning about. After reading the story with your child, encourage him or her to read it to you. Then make a list of objects in your living room and talk about the sounds at the beginning of each object name.

Harcourt

8

Directions: Help children cut and fold the book.
Use with *Teacher's Edition* volume 2, page T339.

TAKE HOME BOOK **45**

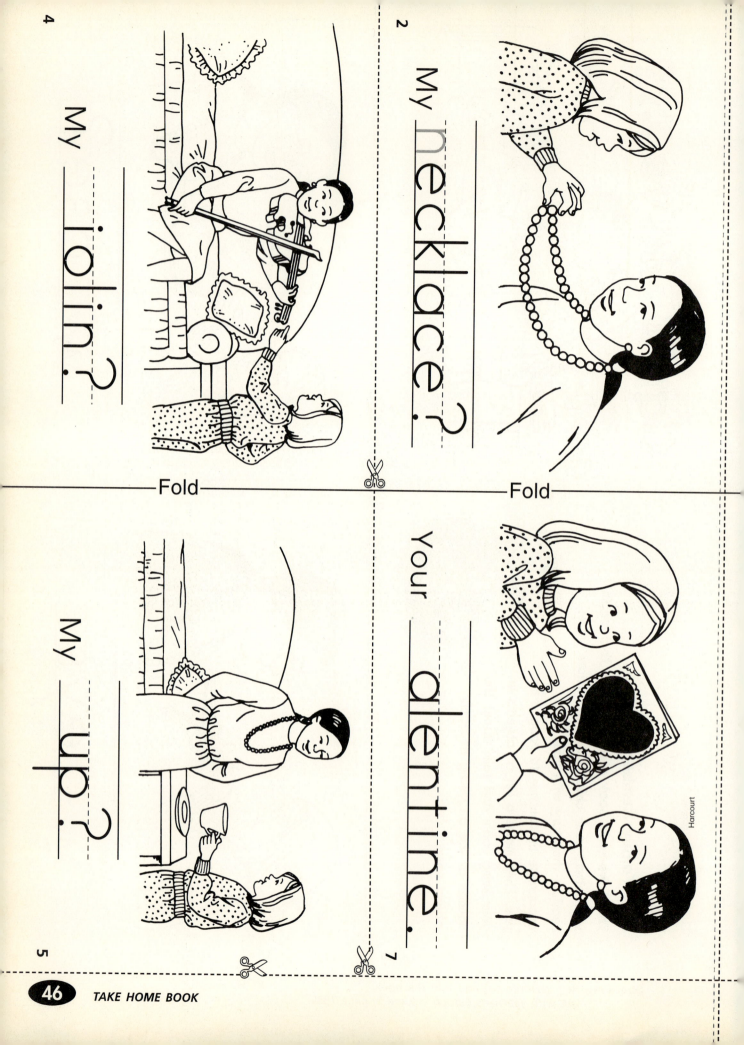

My Garden

by _____

I see a ____ose in it.

See my ____arden?

Dear Family Members,

This Take-Home Book contains words that begin with letters your child is learning about. After reading the story with your child, encourage him or her to read it to you. Then make a list of vegetables that grow in gardens.

Harcourt

Directions: Help children cut and fold the book.
Use with *Teacher's Edition* volume 2, page T393.

TAKE HOME BOOK 49

4

See my _garden_?

2

See my _garden_?

---- Fold ---- ✂ ---- Fold ----

I see a _bird_ in it.

5

I see a _coat_ in it.

7

50 TAKE HOME BOOK

The Surprise

by _____

It is a __an__.

3

Dear Family Members,

This Take-Home Book contains words that begin with letters your child is learning about. After reading the story with your child, encourage him or her to read it to you. Then play a guessing game by taking turns putting an object into a box and giving clues about it.

Harcourt

What is in the __ox__?

Directions: Help children cut and fold the book.
Use with *Teacher's Edition* volume 2, page T435.

TAKE HOME BOOK

Page 2

What is in the garage?

Page 3

It is a amster!

Harcourt

Page 4

What is in the an?

Page 5

It is a ox.

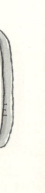

TAKE HOME BOOK

by _____

It is my _____ upcake.

3

Dear Family Members,
This Take-Home Book contains words that end with letters your child is learning about. After reading the story with your child, encourage him or her to read it to you. Then make a list of the rhyming words in the story and have your child name some more rhyming words.

Harcourt

8

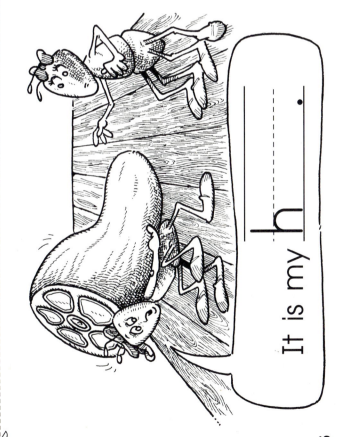

It is my h_____.

Directions: Help children cut and fold the book.
Use with *Teacher's Edition* volume 2, page T467.

TAKE HOME BOOK 53

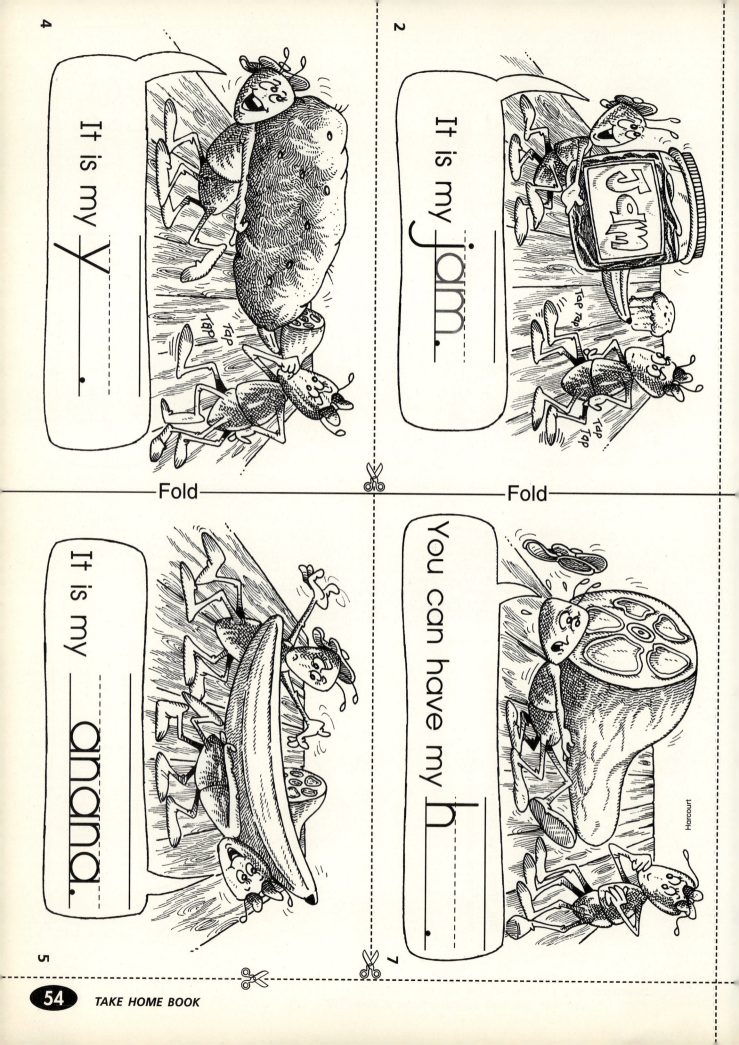

The Missing Cap

by _____

Look on your _____ ap.

3

Dear Family Members,

This Take-Home Book contains words that end with letters your child is learning about. After reading the story with your child, encourage him or her to read it to you. Then talk about what to do if you lose something.

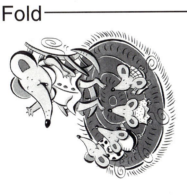

Harcourt

8

Can you see my c_____ ?

6

Directions: Help children cut and fold the book.
Use with *Teacher's Edition* volume 2, page T491.

TAKE HOME BOOK 55

2

Can you see my cap?

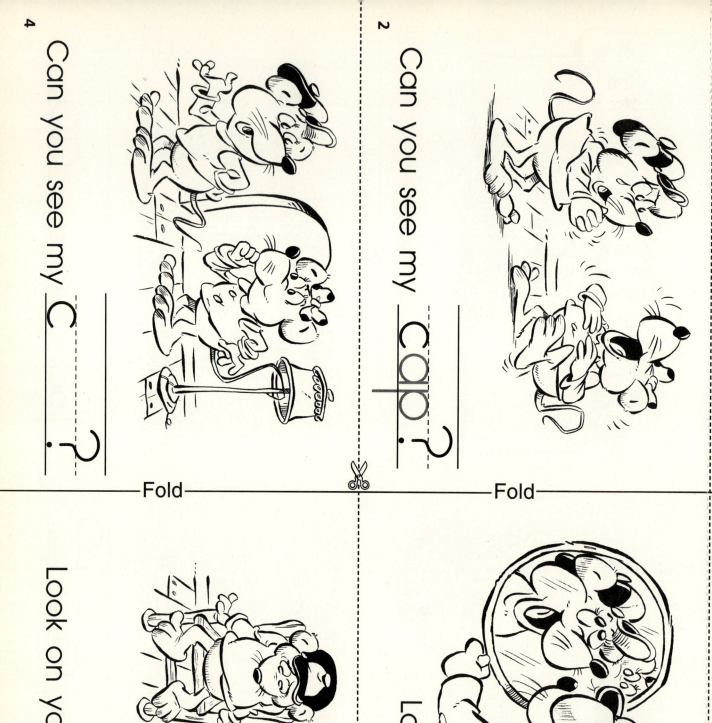

Look!

4

Can you see my c___?

Look on your ap.

56 TAKE HOME BOOK

THE BOAT TRIP

by _____

Where is the C_____?

Where is the _____abbit?

Dear Family Members,
This Take-Home Book contains words that begin and end with letters your child is learning about. After reading the story with your child, encourage him or her to read it to you. Then talk about different kinds of boats you might see on the ocean.

Harcourt

Directions: Help children cut and fold the book.
Use with *Teacher's Edition* volume 2, page T535.

TAKE HOME BOOK

4

Where is the __og__?

2

Where is the __rat__?

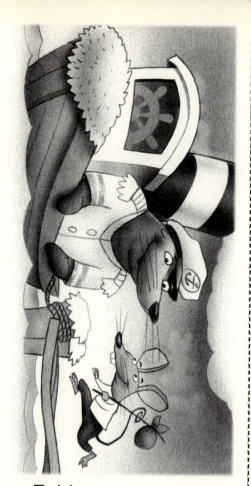

— Fold —

— Fold —

Where is the __oat__?

Where is the __ox__?

7

5

58 TAKE HOME BOOK

The Fish

by _____

I had a __ish.

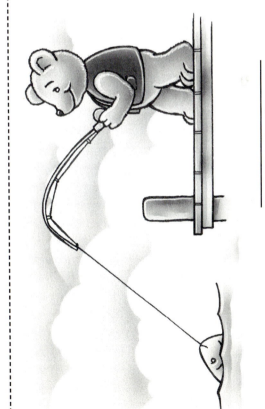

I had a __ail.

Dear Family Members,
This Take-Home Book contains words that begin and end with letters your child is learning about. After reading the story with your child, encourage him or her to read it to you. Then make a list of different animals that live in the ocean.

Harcourt

Directions: Help children cut and fold the book.
Use with *Teacher's Edition* volume 2, page T565.

TAKE HOME BOOK

4

I had a ___orm.

2

I had a ___pole.

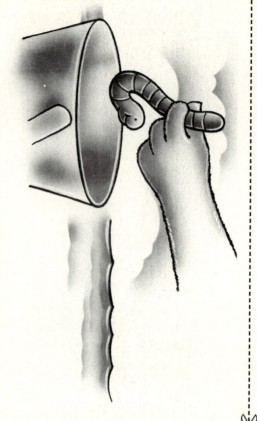

— Fold — ✂ Fold —

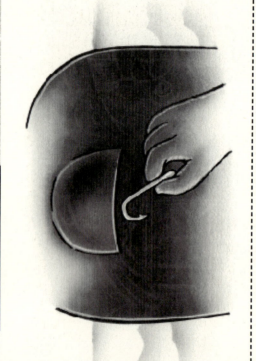

Look at that ___ish!

I had a ___ook.

5   7

60 TAKE HOME BOOK

Look at that!

by _____

Dear Family Members,

This Take-Home Book contains words that begin and end with letters your child is learning about. After reading the story with your child, encourage him or her to read it to you. Then make up stories about an adventurous boat trip.

Harcourt

8

Pat, look at that _____ oat.

3

Tam, look at that _____ et.

6

Directions: Help children cut and fold the book.
Use with *Teacher's Edition* volume 2, page T589.

TAKE HOME BOOK **61**

2

Tam, look at that f_ish.

4

Tam, look at that ave.

Pat, look at that!

Pat, look at that _ird.

5

62 TAKE HOME BOOK

Name _____

M m

Molly Mouse makes muffins.
Molly Mouse cooks meat.
Molly Mouse makes _____.
Then Molly Mouse can eat.

LETTER AND SOUND CHART 1 　　　　　Teacher's Resource Book

F f

Fancy fish go to the fair.
Fancy fish have fun.
They ride the fabulous Ferris wheel
Until the day is done.

Name _____

B b

Bear bounced a ball.

Bird wanted to play.

Bee came buzzing by

And buzzed them both away.

LETTER AND SOUND CHART 3

S s

Sammy Seal sells soup.

Sammy Seal sells soap.

Sammy Seal sells _____.

In the supermarket.

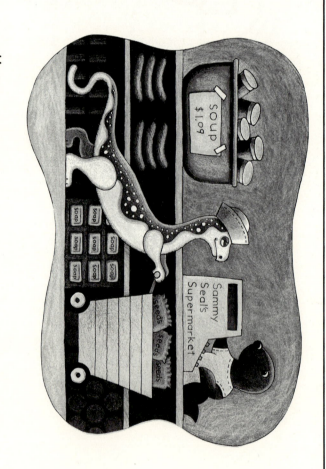

Jj

A jellyfish juggles
Jars of jelly.
When he's done,
One by one,
He puts them in his belly.

LETTER AND SOUND CHART 5

Name _____

P p

Penguin had a party.
All her friends were there—
Porcupine and _____,
Peacock and Polar Bear.

Name _____

H h

Hippo has a hat,
Hippo has a hammer,
Hippo has a _____,
Here inside his house.

LETTER AND SOUND CHART 7

Teacher's Resource Book

69

D d

Danny Duck dives for donuts.
Dolly Duck dives off a tree.
Doddy Duck dives for _____.
But Dudley Duck dives on me!

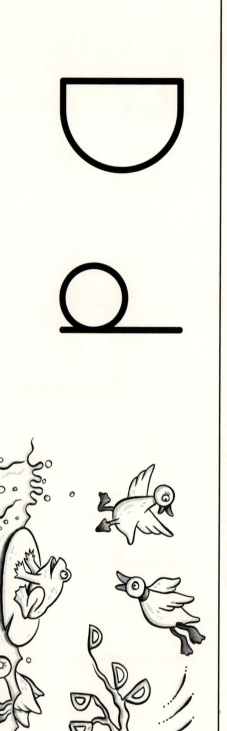

Name _____

C c

Cat calls Camel,
Camel calls Cow,
Cow calls _____,
The cake is ready now!

LETTER AND SOUND CHART 9

A a

Anteater asked Alligator
To make a fancy stew.
He cooked up ants and apricots—
An apple, and a shoe!

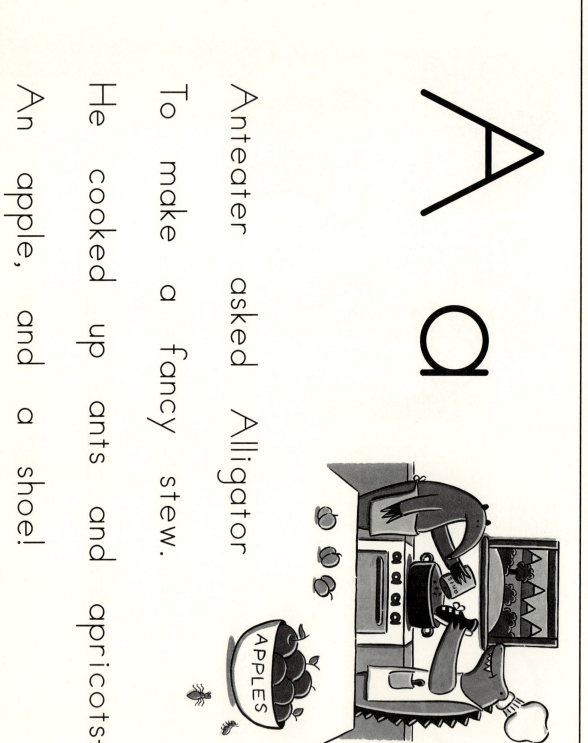

Name _____

Tt

Tiny Turtle drinks tea.

Tiny Turtle eats toast.

Tiny Turtle likes tacos

And _____ the most!

LETTER AND SOUND CHART 11

Teacher's Resource Book

E e

Elephant is an engineer
On Engine Number 9.
Every day he has an egg
And thinks his lunch is fine.

Name _____

Y y

Yak has a yellow yo-yo.

Yak knits with yellow yarn.

Yak eats some yummy yogurt.

Yes—in her yellow barn!

LETTER AND SOUND CHART 13

Name _____

O o

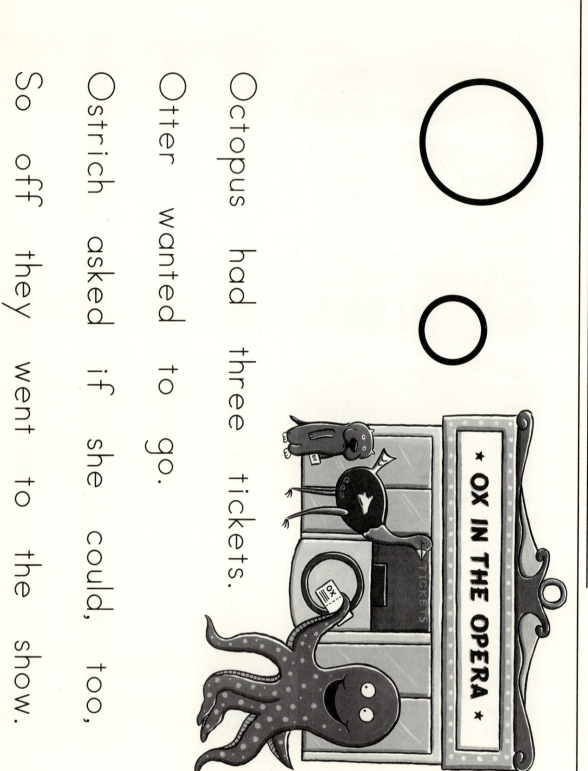

Octopus had three tickets.
Otter wanted to go.
Ostrich asked if she could, too,
So off they went to the show.

Name _____

Z z

Zig zag,
Play tag.
Zebras zip and zoom
At the zoo.

LETTER AND SOUND CHART 15

Teacher's Resource Book 77

K k

Koala went to see the king.
She met a kangaroo.
He kissed Koala in the kitchen.
The king kissed her, too!

Name _____

I i

Iguana stew, just for you.
In go some inchworms,
In goes some glue,
In my iguana stew.

LETTER AND SOUND CHART 17   Teacher's Resource Book

Name _____

W w

Wish, wash,
My gosh,
Walrus washes
In his washing machine.

U u

Up goes a kite,
Up goes a plane,
Up go your umbrellas
Whenever there is rain.

LETTER AND SOUND CHART 19

Ll

Lamb has a lunch box.
What did she pack?
Lettuce and lemonade
For her lunchtime snack.

V v

Vulture packed vegetables,
Vulture packed a vest,
Vulture packed _____,
And drove away in her van.

LETTER AND SOUND CHART 21

N n

My name is Nelly Newt.
My nana says I'm cute.
She never minds if noodles
Get on my nice new shirt.

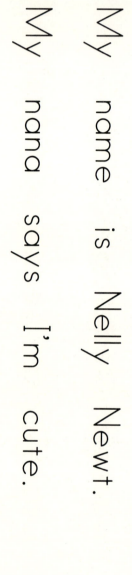

Name _____

G g

Wiggle, giggle,
Geese in the sun.
Waggle, gaggle,
Oh, what fun!

LETTER AND SOUND CHART 23

Name _____

R r

Run, rabbit!
Run, raccoon!
Run, reindeer!
Come back soon!

86 Teacher's Resource Book   LETTER AND SOUND CHART 24

Name _____

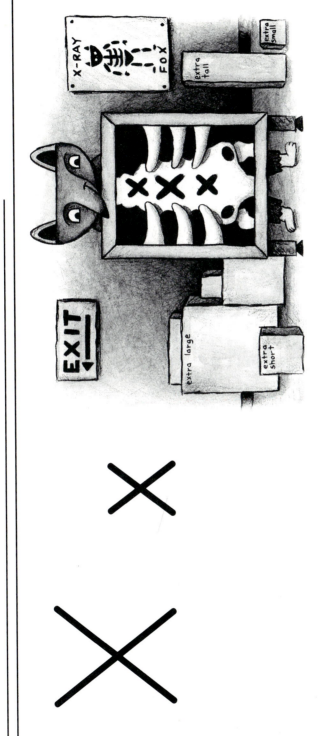

Can you find the x in fox,

X-ray, exit, and in box?,

Extra large and extra small,

Extra short and extra tall?

LETTER AND SOUND CHART 25   Teacher's Resource Book

Q q

Quiet, quiet, quiet,
Don't make a peep!
Queen is under the quilt
Fast asleep.

Name _____

The Alphabet Song

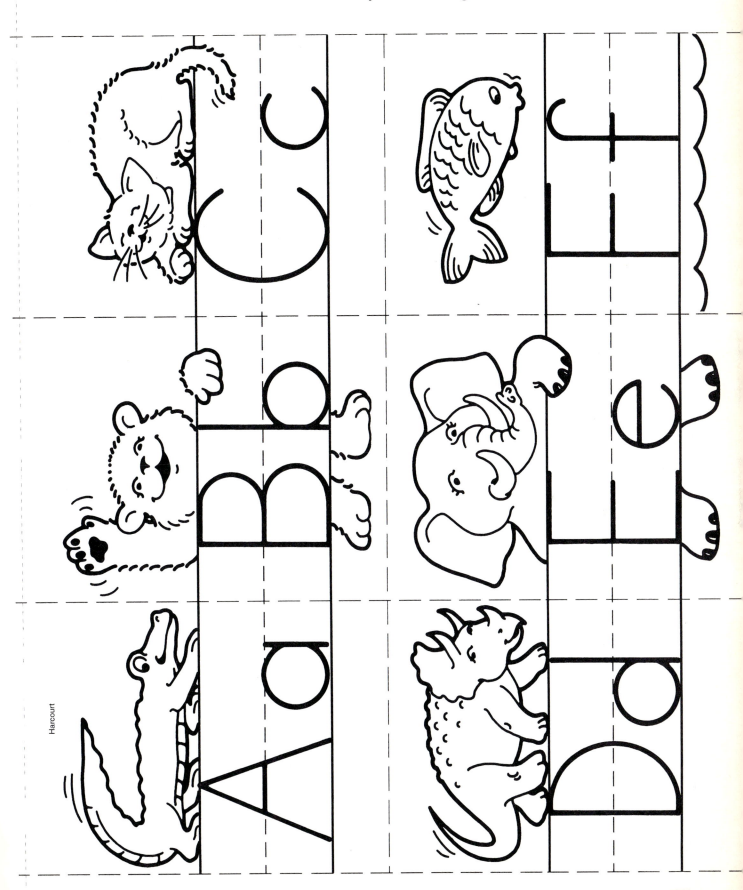

CHARACTER CUTOUTS — Getting to Know You 89

Name _____

The Alphabet Song

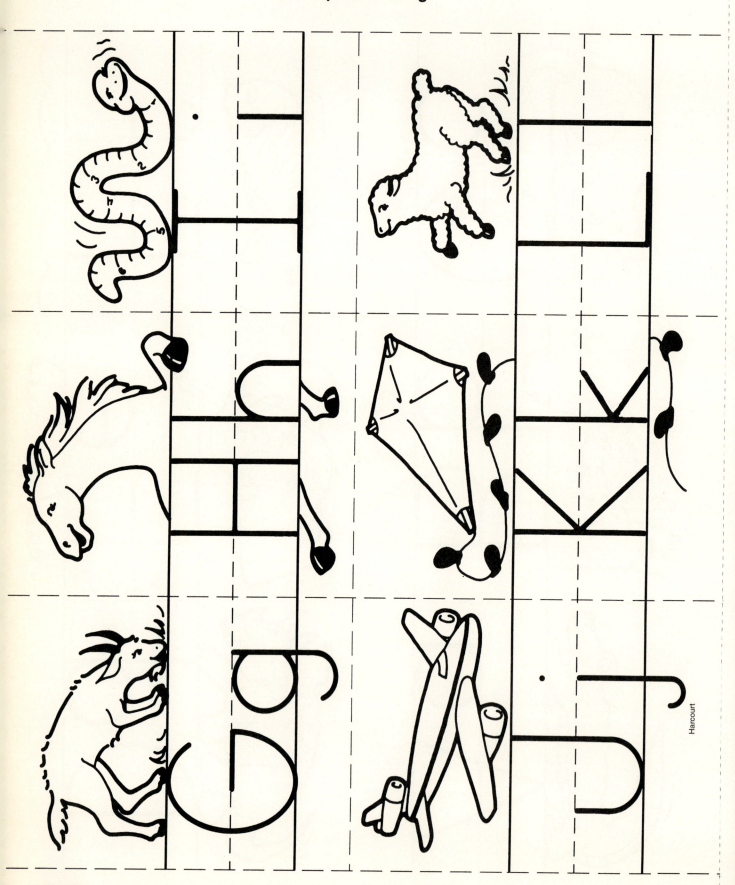

90 Getting to Know You CHARACTER CUTOUTS

Name _____

The Alphabet Song

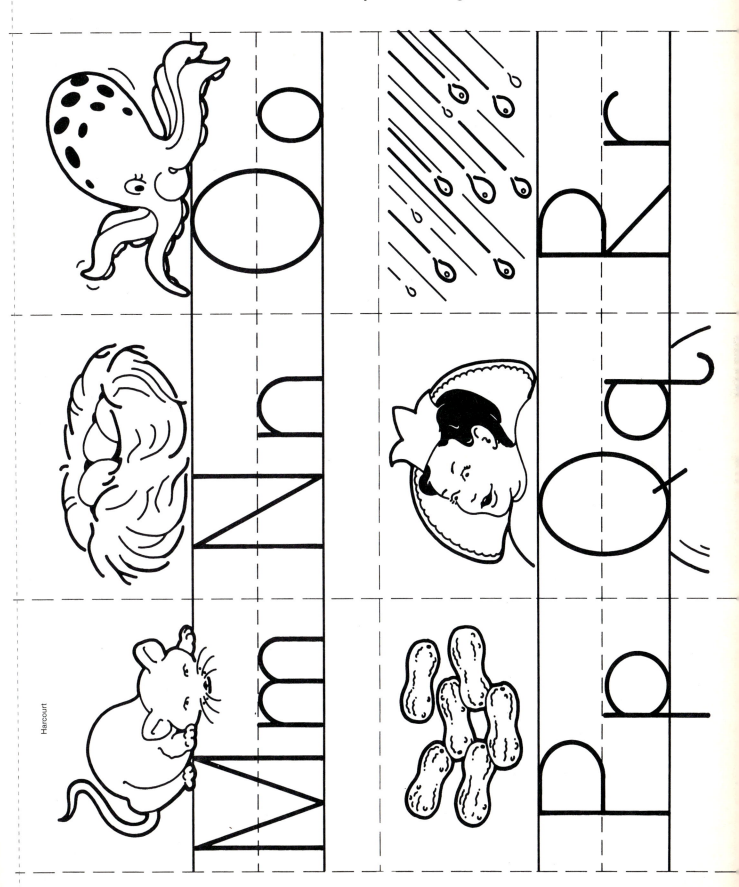

CHARACTER CUTOUTS

Getting to Know You

Name _____

The Alphabet Song

92 Getting to Know You

CHARACTER CUTOUTS

Name _____

The Alphabet Song

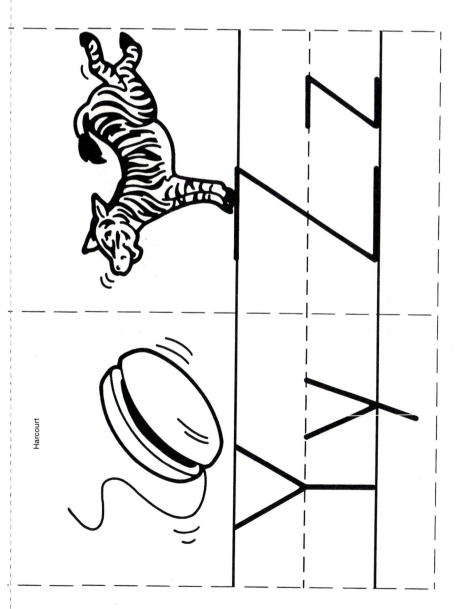

CHARACTER CUTOUTS

Getting to Know You 93

Name _____

The Hare and the Tortoise

94 I Am Special

CHARACTER CUTOUTS

Name _____

Bought Me a Cat

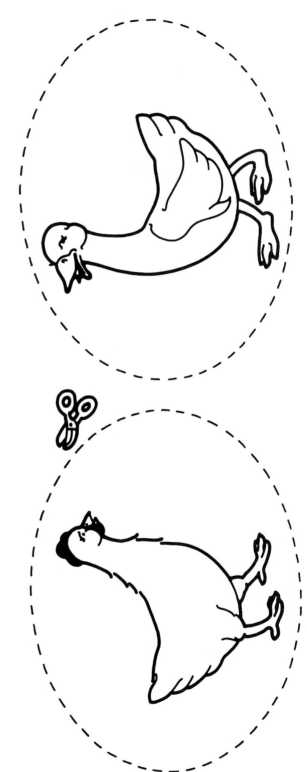

CHARACTER CUTOUTS   Animals I Like

Name _____

Bought Me a Cat

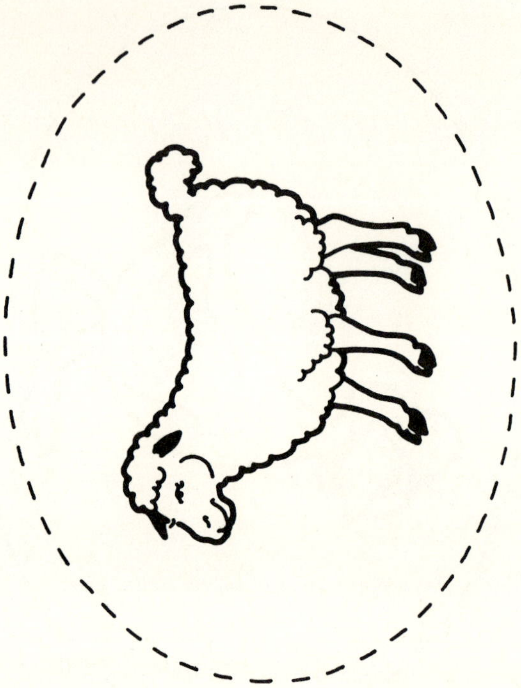

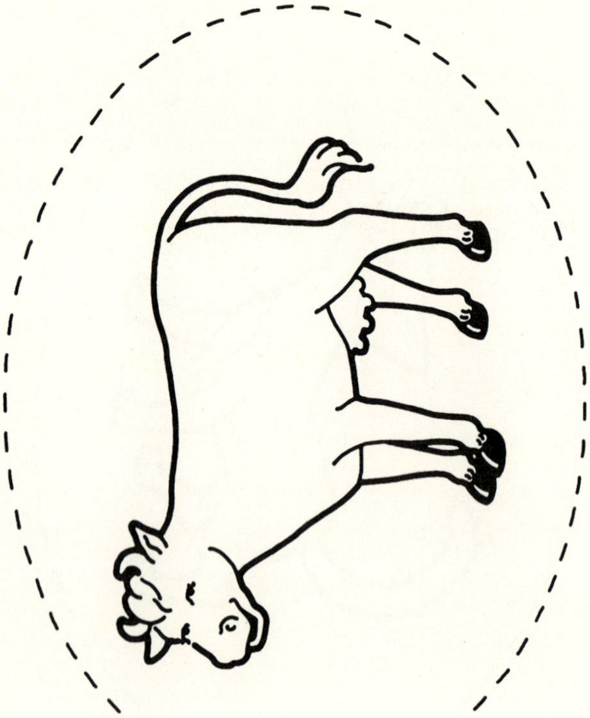

96 Animals I Like

CHARACTER CUTOUTS

Name _____

The Gingerbread Man

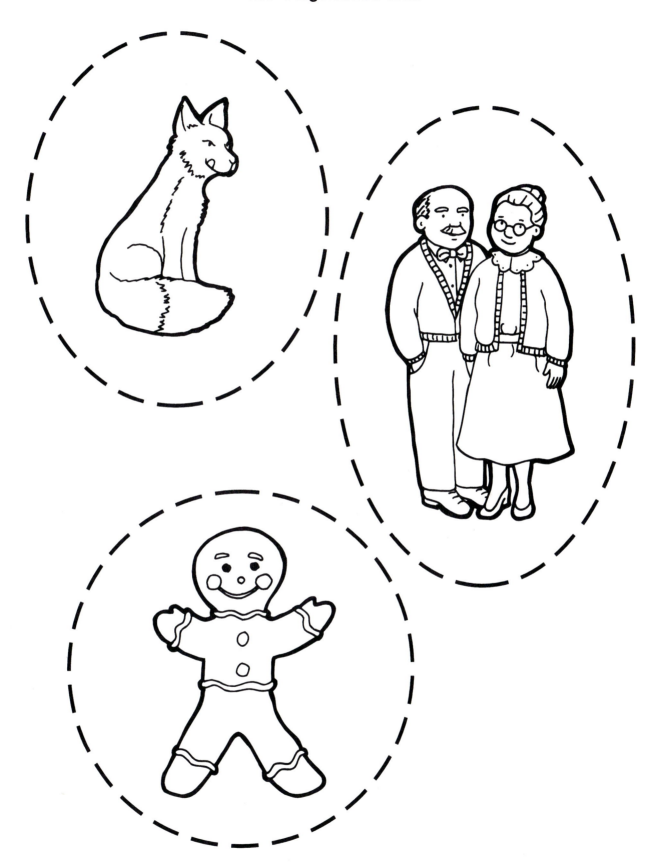

CHARACTER CUTOUTS

Around the Table

97

Name _____

The Gingerbread Man

98 Around the Table

CHARACTER CUTOUTS

Name _____

The Three Billy-Goats Gruff

CHARACTER CUTOUTS   Family and Friends   **99**

Name _____

Franklin in the Dark

100 Watch Me Grow

CHARACTER CUTOUTS

Name _____

Franklin in the Dark

CHARACTER CUTOUTS

Watch Me Grow

Name _____

Mother, Mother, I Want Another

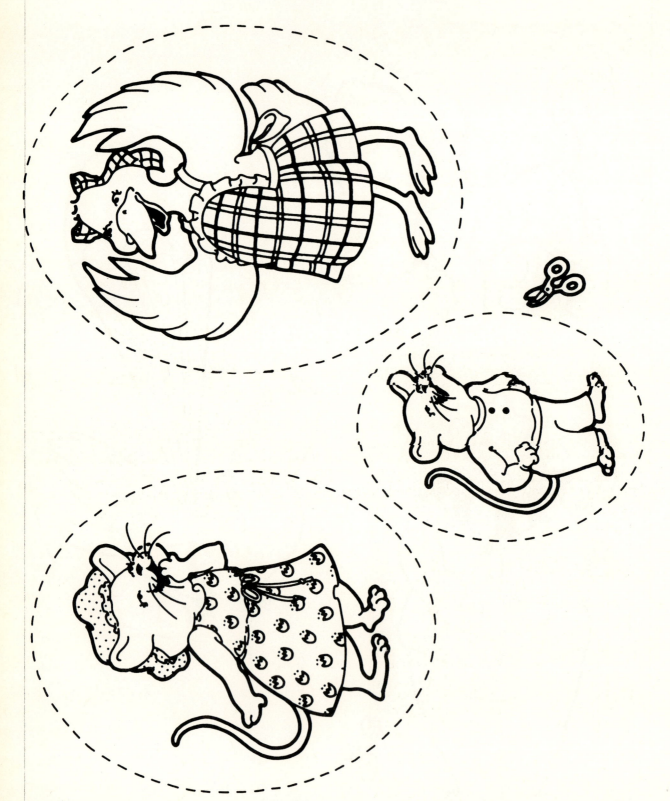

102 Animal Families   CHARACTER CUTOUTS

Name _____

Mother, Mother, I Want Another

CHARACTER CUTOUTS

Animal Families

103

Name _____

Coyote and Turtle

Silly Business

CHARACTER CUTOUTS

Name _____

Henny Penny

CHARACTER CUTOUTS　　　　Animal Adventures　105

Name _____

Henny Penny

106 Animal Adventures

CHARACTER CUTOUTS

Name _____

The Three Little Pigs

CHARACTER CUTOUTS

Around the Town

107

Name _____

**Anansi and the Biggest, Sweetest Melon
An African Tale**

108 Growing Things   CHARACTER CUTOUTS

Name _____

**Anansi and the Biggest, Sweetest Melon
An African Tale**

CHARACTER CUTOUTS

Growing Things

109

Name _____

My Pet Spider

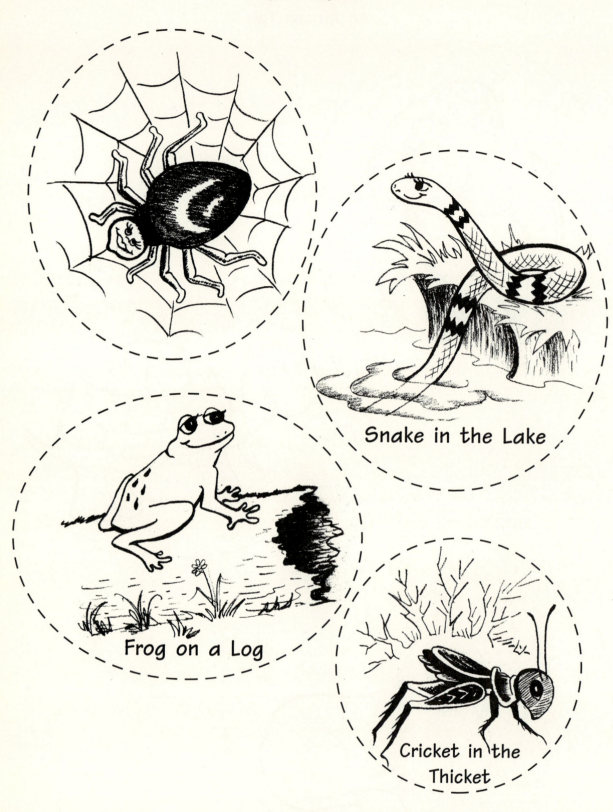

Snake in the Lake

Frog on a Log

Cricket in the Thicket

Bug Surprises

CHARACTER CUTOUTS

Name _____

My Pet Spider

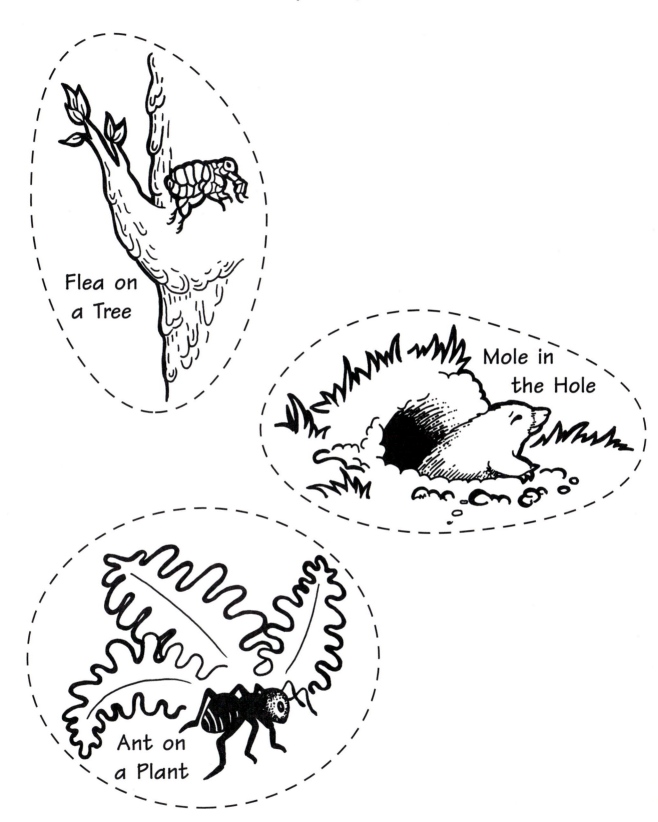

Flea on a Tree

Mole in the Hole

Ant on a Plant

CHARACTER CUTOUTS

Bug Surprises

Name _____

If You Ever

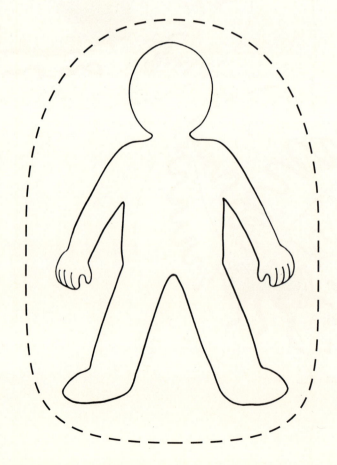

112 Under the Ocean

CHARACTER CUTOUTS

DRAMA

Moo Moo, Brown Cow

Sort and Tell

1. Get:
   story cutouts

   flannel board

   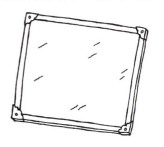

2. Put in place.

3. Tell a story.

BIG BOOK ACTIVITY CARD 1   Teacher's Resource Book

ART

From Anne to Zach

Who Am I?

1. Get: scissors, grocery bag, glue, scraps

2. Cut.

3. Decorate.

4. Wear.

114 Teacher's Resource Book

BIG BOOK ACTIVITY CARD 2

MICE SQUEAK, WE SPEAK
MAKE A HAND PRINT

1. Get:

   tray of paint

   paper

   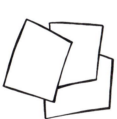

2. Dip.

3. Press.

4. Compare.

TEN CATS HAVE HATS

Sort and Count

1. Get:

toy cars   toy trucks

crayons   paper

2. Sort.

3. Count.

3 cars

4 trucks

4. Arrange.

116 Teacher's Resource Book   BIG BOOK ACTIVITY CARD 4

SCIENCE

PEANUT BUTTER AND JELLY

Healthful Snacks

1. Get: paper plate

scissors

 magazines   glue

2. Cut out.

3. Glue.

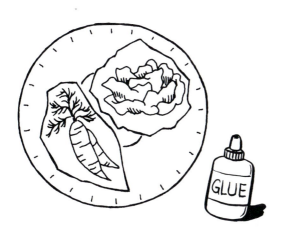

4. Share.

BIG BOOK ACTIVITY CARD 5   Teacher's Resource Book   117

FIVE LITTLE DUCKS

"Five Little Ducks" Puppet Show

Get:

paper   craft sticks   crayons

glue   scissors

1.

Draw pictures of ducks.

2.

Cut out the ducks. Glue them on sticks.

3. Retell the story.

WRITING

Pass the Fritters, Critters
Here's What I Can Do

1. Get:

crayons

paper
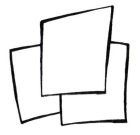

2. Draw.

3. Share.

4. Save.

BIG BOOK ACTIVITY CARD 7

Teacher's Resource Book 119

LITTLE ELEPHANT
ANIMAL FAMILY

1. Get:

rocks   hand lens

paint    paintbrush

2. Look.

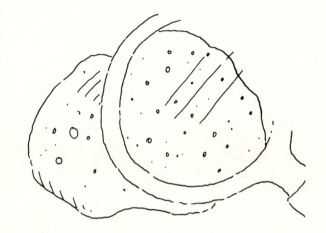

3. Sort.

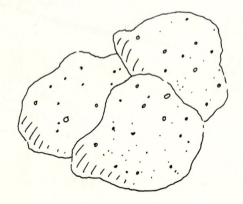

4. Paint.

MUSIC

MOUSE MESS

Crackle-sweep Maracas

1. Get:

2 small paper bags   dried beans

paint   scissors
paintbrushes

2. Paint.

3. Add beans and tie.

4. Shake!

BIG BOOK ACTIVITY CARD 9

WRITING

WALKING THROUGH THE JUNGLE

Adventure Stories

Get:

 magazines  greeting cards   scissors glue paper

1. Cut.

2. Sort.

3. Write.

4. Share.

122 Teacher's Resource Book

BIG BOOK ACTIVITY CARD 10

WRITING

PEOPLE WORKING
Make a Mailbox

1. Get:
tissue box   crayons

index cards   envelope

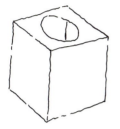
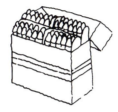

2. Write your name and address.

3. Glue on your name.

4. Send a letter.

BIG BOOK ACTIVITY CARD 11   Teacher's Resource Book

SCIENCE

Jasper's Beanstalk

Grow a Beanstalk

Get:
beans   milk cartons   soil

1. Put in soil and beans.

2. Put more soil.

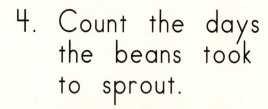

3. Water when dry.

4. Count the days the beans took to sprout.

124 Teacher's Resource Book   BIG BOOK ACTIVITY CARD 12

COOKING

Look Closer
Ants on a Log

Get:

celery   peanut butter   knife   raisins

1. Scrub.

2. Cut.

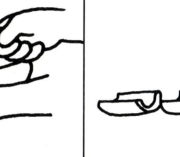

3. Spread.

4. Count and add five raisins.

BIG BOOK ACTIVITY CARD 13   Teacher's Resource Book   125

SPLASH IN THE OCEAN!

Wibble Wobble Hoops

1. Get:

cardboard strip

stapler   glue

yarn

Splash in the Ocean! cassette

2. Staple.

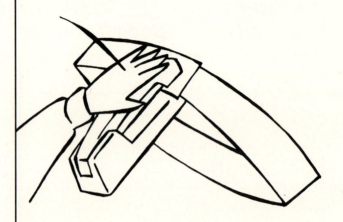

3. Add trim.

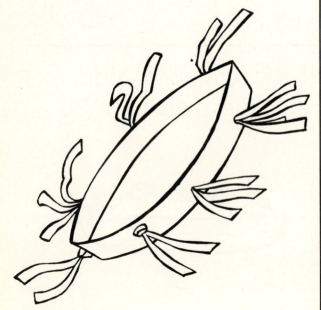

4. Dance!

126 Teacher's Resource Book   BIG BOOK ACTIVITY CARD 14

Name _____

BLUE RIBBON AWARD

1. COLOR.
2. CUT.
3. WEAR.

Teacher's Resource Book 127

Name _____

Wristband Messages

1. Reproduce and cut out. Cut the slits.
2. Write a message on the shape.
3. Insert the tail through the slits to close.
4. Place around child's wrist and close.

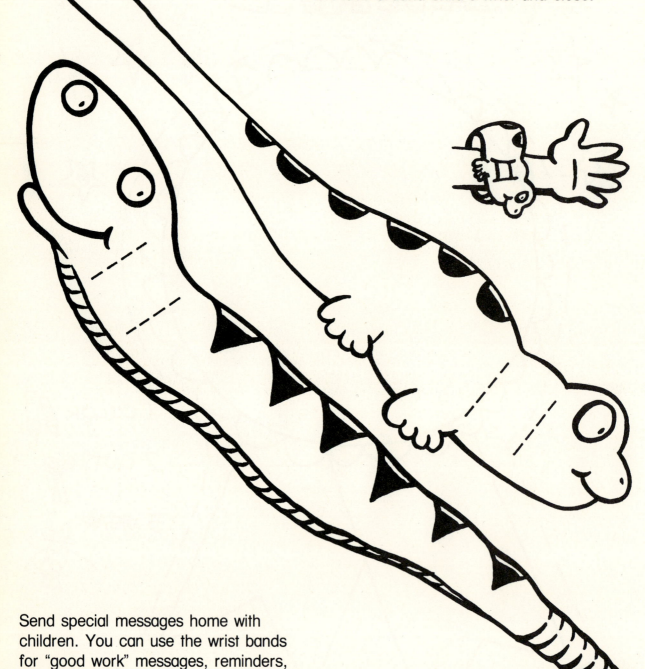

Send special messages home with children. You can use the wrist bands for "good work" messages, reminders, and more!

Teacher's Resource Book

Name _____

STORY STAGE

① Write about or draw three scenes from a story.

② Cut on the dotted lines.

③ Pull the strip through the slits. Tell the story.

Teacher's Resource Book   129

Name _____

My Story Book

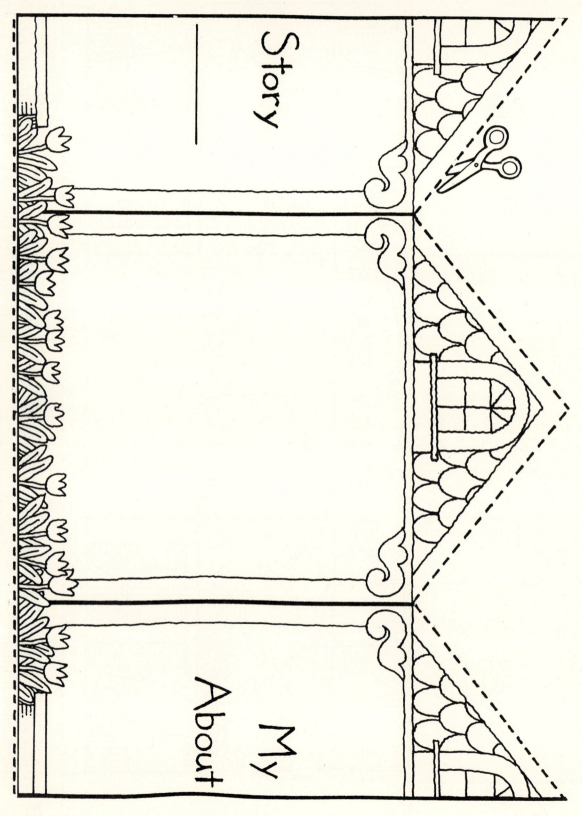

130 Teacher's Resource Book

Name _____

Paper Plate Puppets

Make multiple copies of this sheet, or have children trace the puppet pieces. Have children cut out the pieces, paste them onto small paper plates, and tape a large craft stick to the back of each. Encourage children to add details such as feathers, fur, eyebrows, and whiskers to their puppets. Children can use the puppets to retell stories and to create new versions.

Teacher's Resource Book

Name _____

Racetrack Game Board

1. Make two copies. 2. Cut out. 3. Glue onto a file folder.

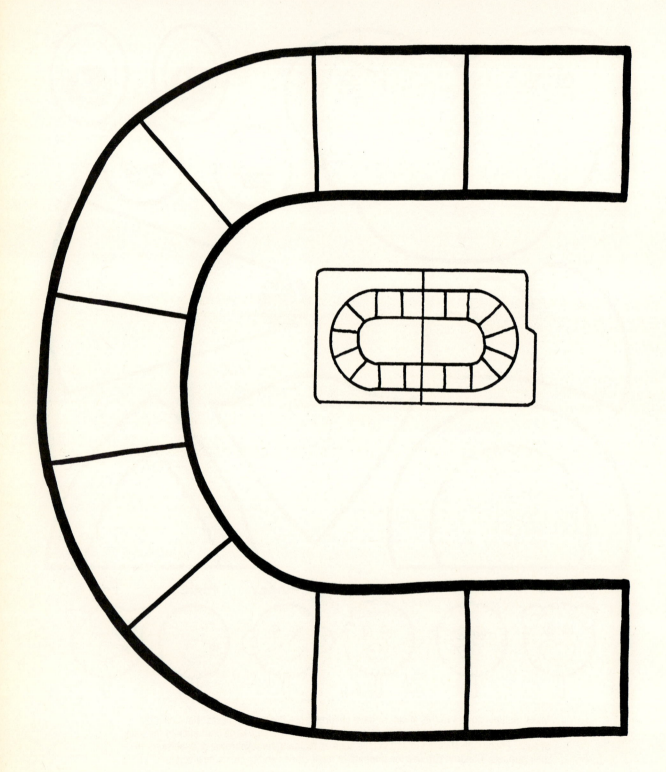

132 Teacher's Resource Book

Name _____

Mountain Game Board

1. Cut out.   3. Glue onto construction paper.

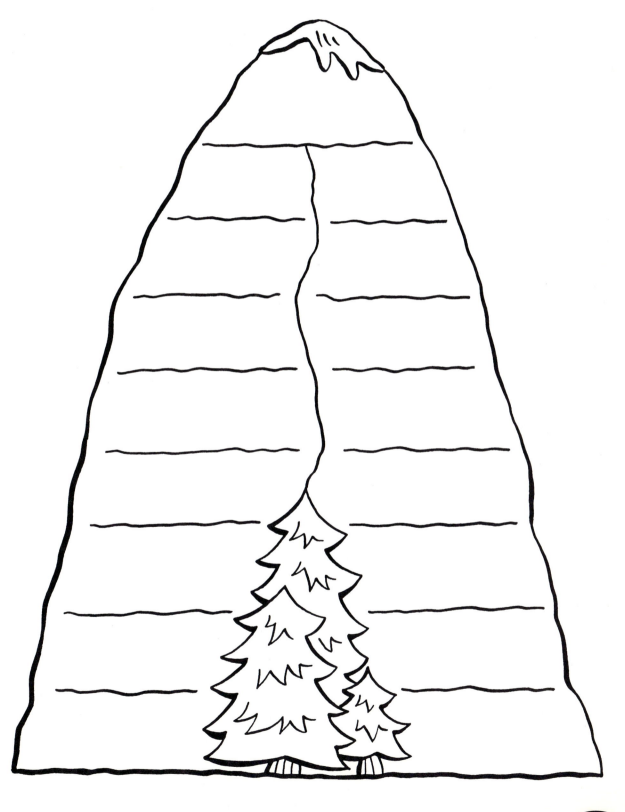

Harcourt

Teacher's Resource Book   **133**

Name _____

S-Shape Game Board (left side)

1. Make a copy of both S-Shape Game Boards.
2. Cut out.   3. Glue onto a file folder.

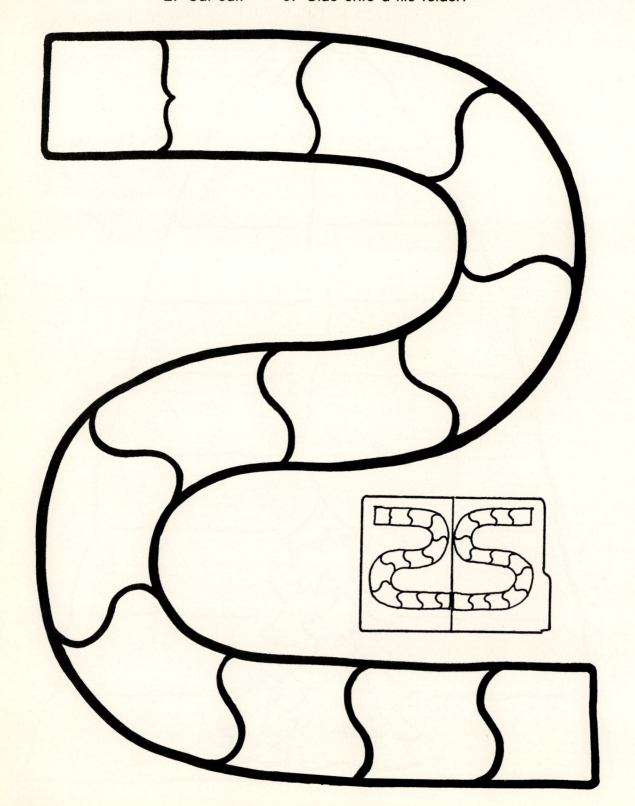

134 Teacher's Resource Book

Name _____

S-Shape Game Board (right side)

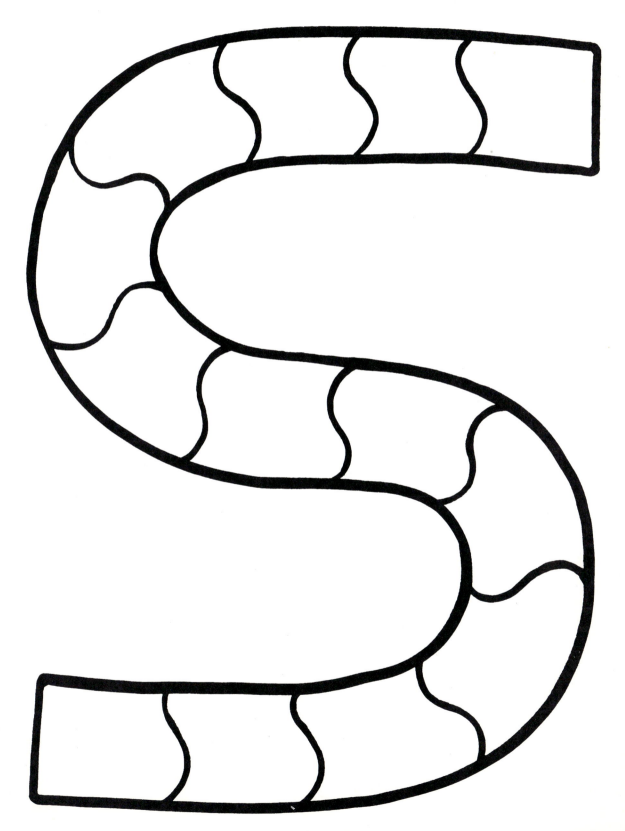

Name _____

Loop Game Board (left side)

1. Make a copy of both Loop Game Boards.
2. Cut out.   3. Glue onto a file folder.

Name _____

Loop Game Board (right side)

Teacher's Resource Book 137

Name _____

Dot Game Board

1. Cut out.   2. Glue onto construction paper.

138 Teacher's Resource Book

Spinners

1. Cut out a wheel and glue it onto thick paper.
2. Put on a paper clip with a brad.

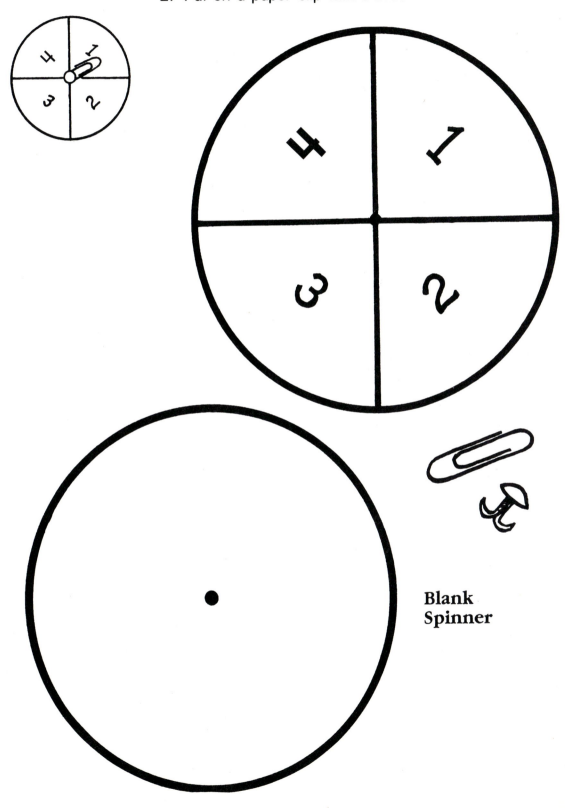

Blank Spinner

Teacher's Resource Book

Name _____

9 and 12-Square Grid

140 Teacher's Resource Book

Name _____

16-Square Grid

Name _____

Finger Puppets

1. Cut.

2. Draw or write.

3. Tape.

4. Wear.

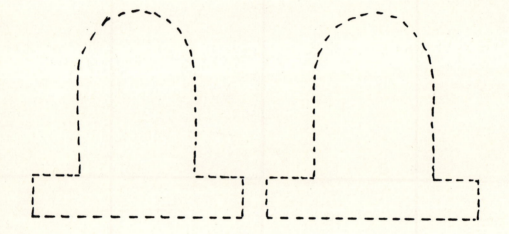

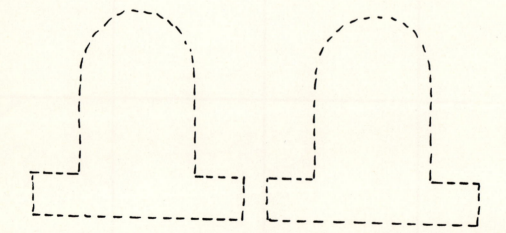

Name _____

Word Wheel

1. Cut out each wheel.   2. Attach with a brad.

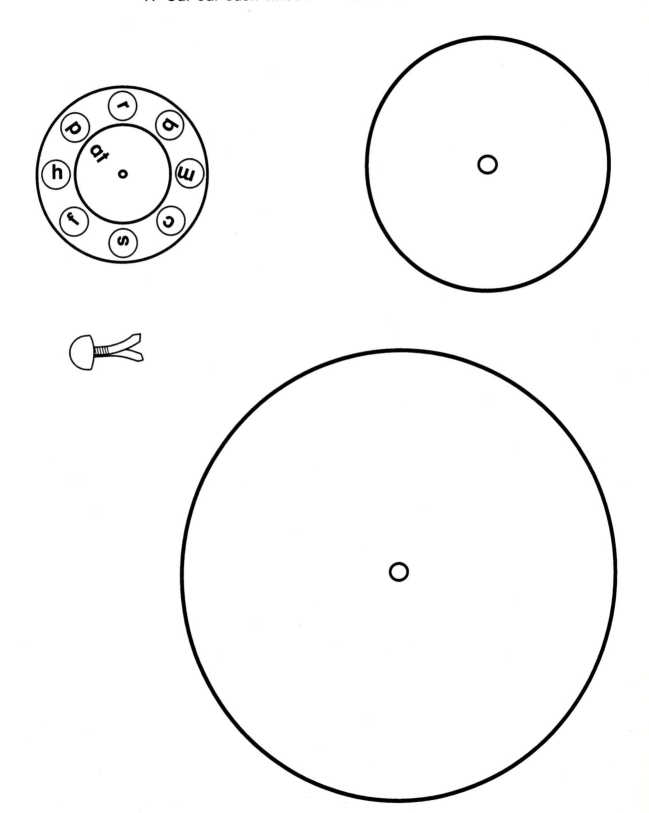

Teacher's Resource Book   143

Name _____

Wordscope

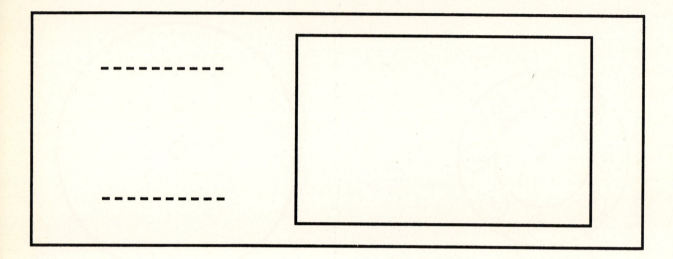

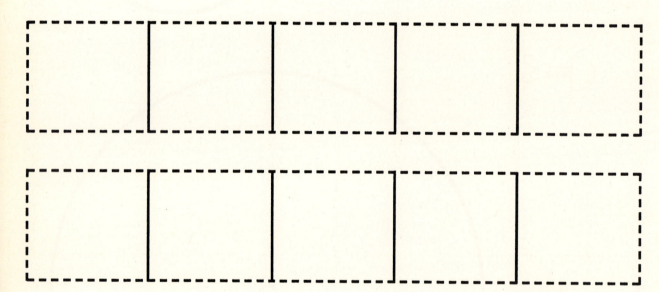

Cut out the box and the strips. Cut slits in the box on the dotted lines. Write a phonogram in the box. Write letters that stand for initial sounds on the strip. Pull and read the words.

Teacher's Resource Book

Name _____

Pop-Up Book

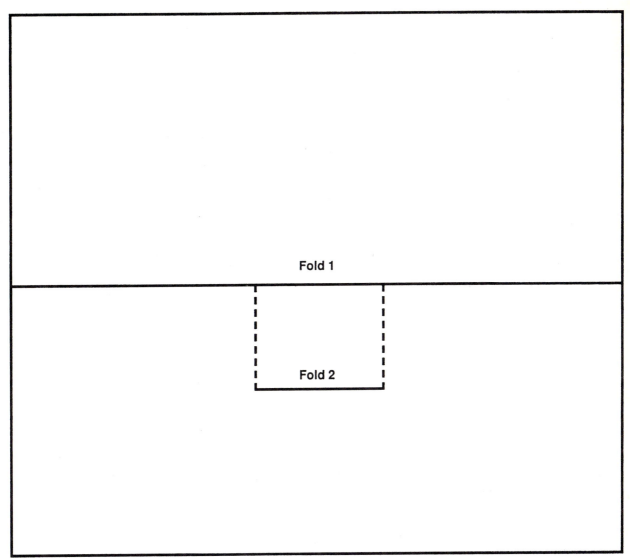

1. Cut out the book. Fold the book in half.

2. Cut on the dotted lines through both layers.

3. Fold on the solid lines. Open and refold so the box will pop out.

4. Glue it inside a cover.

5. Glue a picture on the pop-up.

Teacher's Resource Book

Name _____

Step-Page Book

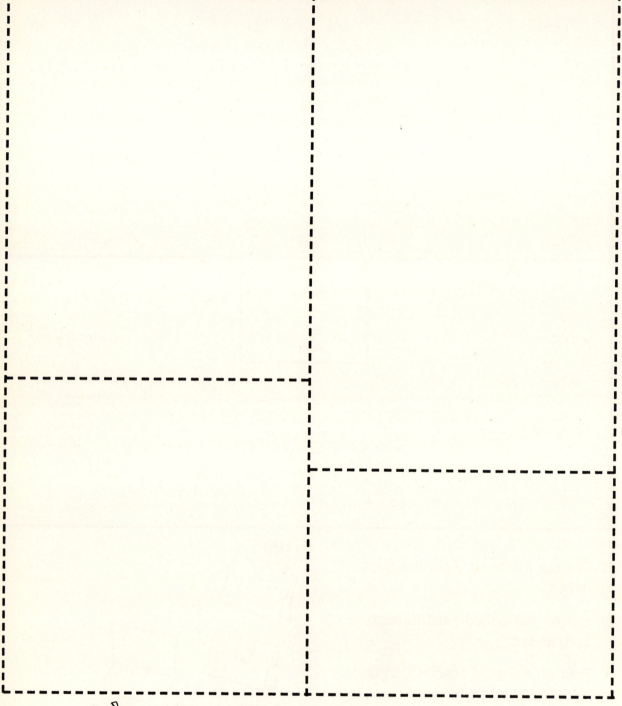

1. Cut out the four pages.
2. Lay the pages one on top of the other.
3. Bind the pages at the top.

Name _____

Pull-Out Book

- - - - - - - - - - - - -

   1. Cut out as many pages and pull-out tabs as you need. Cut the slit on each page.

   2. Make a cover from a folded sheet of paper.

   3. Staple the book together.

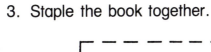

Teacher's Resource Book 147

Name _____

Word Cards

Name _____

Letter Cards (Lowercase)

a	b	c	d	e
f	g	h	i	j
k	l	m	n	o
p	q	r	s	t
u	v	w	x	y
z				

Name _____

Letter Cards (Capital)

A	B	C	D	E
F	G	H	I	J
K	L	M	N	O
P	Q	R	S	T
U	V	W	X	Y
Z				

150 Teacher's Resource Book

Name _____

Word Builder

1. Cut out the Word Builder.
2. Fold up the pocket.
3. Staple it on each side.
4. Draw an arrow on the pocket.

Fold.

Teacher's Resource Book

Name _____

Reading Log

Tape the cars together. Fold the book to store it.

Children can make an accordion book to keep a record of books they have read. Make several copies of the train cars to use.

152 Teacher's Resource Book

Name _____

I	a
the	have
you	my

HIGH-FREQUENCY WORD CARDS   Teacher's Resource Book

Name _____

can	in
like	see
what	and

Name _____

your	it
on	is
look	where
that	

HIGH-FREQUENCY WORD CARDS

Teacher's Resource Book